☐ RANGE
OREGON SPOTTED
FROG

☐ RANGE
CHIRICAHUA
LEOPARD FROG

☐ RANGE
AMERICAN TOAD

☐ RANGE
GOPHER FROG

☐ RANGE
PINE BARRENS
TREE FROG

☐ RANGE
CALIFORNIA
RED-LEGGED FROG

A PLACE FOR
FROGS

For Emile, a fellow frog lover
—M. S.

With sincere gratitude to Anita Grien
—H. B.

Published by
PEACHTREE PUBLISHERS
1700 Chattahoochee Avenue
Atlanta, Georgia 30318-2112
www.peachtree-online.com

Book design by Loraine M. Joyner
Composition by Melanie McMahon Ives
Illustrations created in acrylic on cold press illustration board
Title typeset in Nick Curtis's HardlyWorthIt; main text typeset
in Monotype's Century Schoolbook with Apple's Techno initial
capitals; sidebar titles typeset in Apple's Techno; and sidebar
text typeset in Adobe's Optima.

Printed and manufactured in December 2015 by Imago in Singapore
10 9 8 7 6 5 4 3 2 1 (hardcover)
10 9 8 7 6 5 4 3 2 1 (paperback)
Revised Edition

Library of Congress Cataloging-in-Publication Data
Stewart, Melissa.
  A place for frogs / written by Melissa Stewart ; illustrated by
Higgins Bond.
    p. cm.
  ISBN 978-1-56145-901-8 (hardcover)
  ISBN 978-1-56145-902-5 (paperback)
  1. Frogs—Habitat—Juvenile literature. 2. Nature—Effect of
human beings on—Juvenile literature. I. Bond, Higgins, ill. II. Title.
  QL668.E2S745 2010
  597.8'9217—dc22
                        2009024515

A PLACE FOR
FROGS

Written by
Melissa Stewart

Illustrated by
Higgins Bond

PEACHTREE
ATLANTA

Frogs make our world a better place. But sometimes people do things that make it hard for them to live and grow.

A Frog's Life

As frogs grow, they go through four life stages. A female frog lays eggs in a wet place. When a tiny tadpole breaks out, it spends most of its time eating and growing. Soon the tadpole develops legs. Its tail shrinks, and it starts breathing air. When the froglet hops onto land, it grows quickly and loses its tail. Finally, it becomes a full-grown frog and is ready to find a mate.

GREEN FROG

If we work together to help these special creatures,
there will always be a place for frogs.

For frogs to survive, they need to stay safe and healthy. Some tadpoles are harmed by chemicals farmers use to help their crops grow.

When farmers and scientists find new ways
to improve crops, frogs can live and grow.

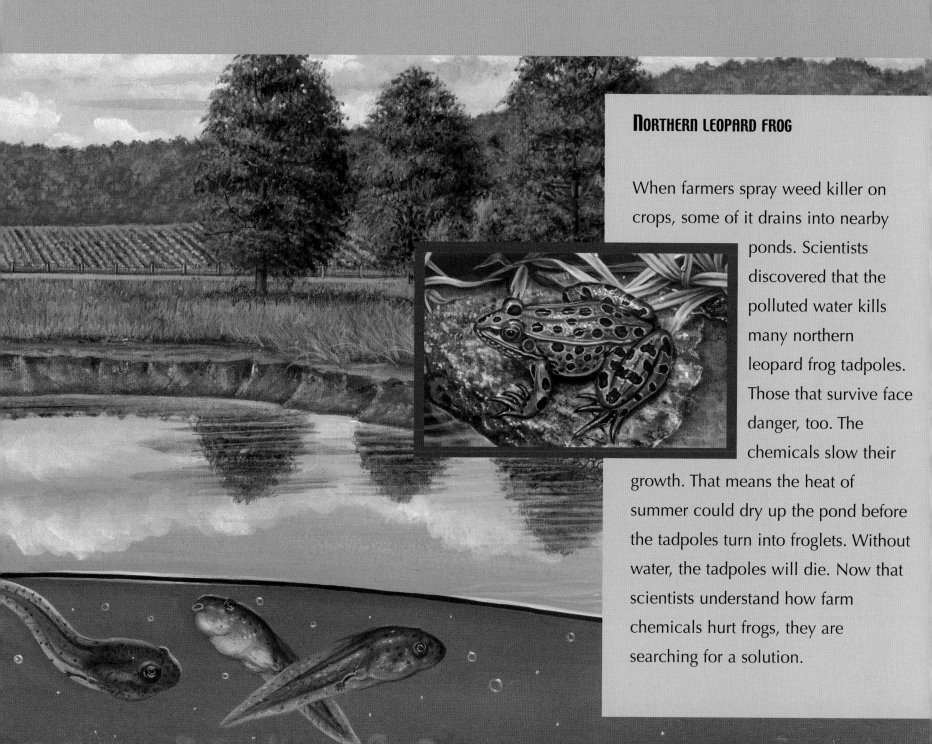

NORTHERN LEOPARD FROG

When farmers spray weed killer on crops, some of it drains into nearby ponds. Scientists discovered that the polluted water kills many northern leopard frog tadpoles. Those that survive face danger, too. The chemicals slow their growth. That means the heat of summer could dry up the pond before the tadpoles turn into froglets. Without water, the tadpoles will die. Now that scientists understand how farm chemicals hurt frogs, they are searching for a solution.

Tadpoles don't stand a chance when people add fish to lakes and ponds.

SIERRA NEVADA
YELLOW-LEGGED FROG

Because the lakes high in the Sierra Nevada Mountains are so beautiful, people thought it would be fun to go fishing there. They added tons of trout to the lakes. Over time, the fish ate most of the yellow-legged tadpoles.

When scientists noticed the problem, they began removing trout from lakes. In 2014, the Sierra Nevada yellow-legged frog was added to the U.S. Endangered Species List. Now scientists are raising tadpoles and releasing froglets into the wild.

TROUT

When people take out the fish, frogs can live and grow.

Some frogs have trouble surviving when people introduce new plants to a natural habitat.

When people grow native plants to feed their horses and cattle, frogs can live and grow.

OREGON SPOTTED FROG

As Americans moved westward in the 1800s, some of them planted reed canary grass to feed their animals. When the thick grass spread into wetlands, Oregon spotted frogs had trouble finding sunny places to lay their eggs. In 2014, the U.S. government decided that the Oregon spotted frog is a threatened species. Now people are working hard to remove reed canary grass, so frogs will have more places to lay their eggs.

Many frogs are dying of a terrible disease caused by a fungus. Some scientists think it spread because people released infected frogs into the wild.

CHIRICAHUA LEOPARD FROG

In the 1990s, Chiricahua leopard frogs suddenly began dying. So did other kinds of frogs. What was killing them? A fungus. But scientists didn't know how it was spreading. In 2013, they realized that African clawed frogs might be to blame.

In the past, many people kept African clawed frogs as pets. Hospital workers used them in tests. Some of the frogs escaped. Others were set free. Scientists think these frogs were infected with the fungus. When they came into contact with other frogs, the fungus spread and turned deadly. This new information may help scientists treat the disease.

CHIRICAHUA LEOPARD FROG

AFRICAN CLAWED FROG

When scientists discover a way to treat the disease, frogs can live and grow.

Many people let their dogs run free when they go hiking in natural areas. But curious dogs can hurt frogs and other small animals.

When hikers keep their dogs on leashes, frogs can live and grow.

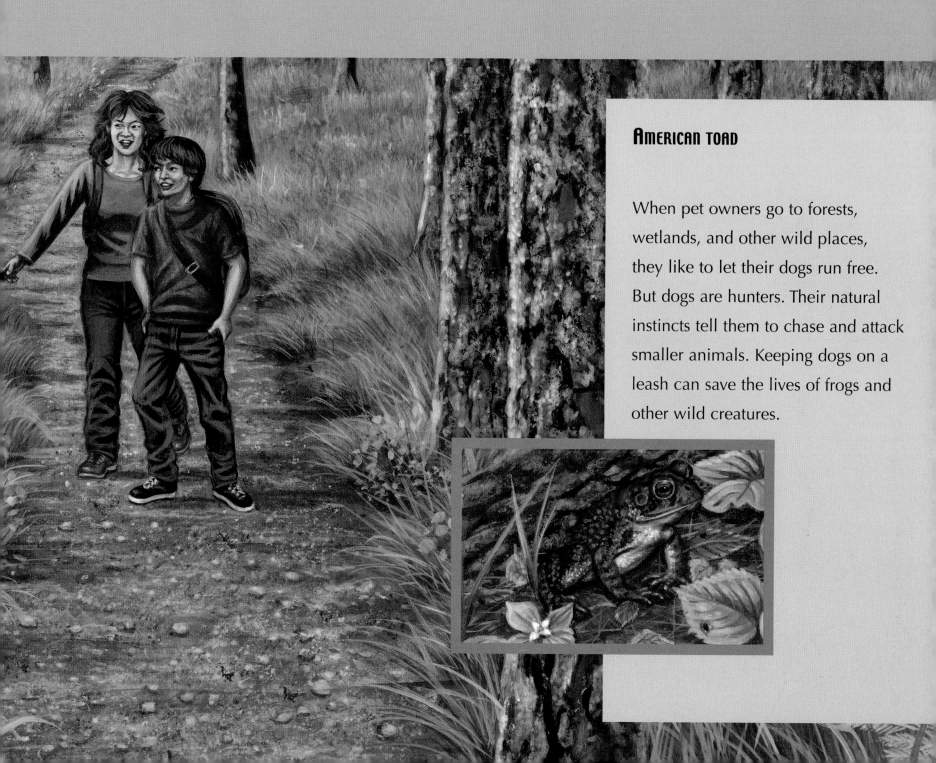

AMERICAN TOAD

When pet owners go to forests, wetlands, and other wild places, they like to let their dogs run free. But dogs are hunters. Their natural instincts tell them to chase and attack smaller animals. Keeping dogs on a leash can save the lives of frogs and other wild creatures.

Some frogs are so beautiful that people like to keep them as pets.

PANAMANIAN GOLDEN FROG

It's against the law to collect
Panamanian golden frogs from their
rainforest home. But some people
do it anyway. They
want to make money
selling the rare,
colorful frogs to
pet stores.

Frogs don't make
good pets. They can't
form a special bond
with people. And they aren't happy
living in our homes. If people stop
buying pet frogs, collectors will leave
Panamanian golden frogs alone.

When people stop catching these colorful
creatures, frogs can live and grow.

Frogs have trouble surviving when their natural homes are destroyed. Many frogs must lay their eggs in temporary pools that dry up in the summer.

When people create new part-time ponds, frogs can live and grow.

EASTERN SPADEFOOT TOAD

As Europeans settled in North America, they changed the land to meet their needs. Some people in Massachusetts filled in temporary ponds as they built homes or created farms. Eventually, eastern spadefoot toads had trouble finding suitable spots to lay their eggs.

From 2011 to 2013, scientists and citizens dug nine new pools at nature centers on Cape Cod, Massachusetts. Now children at local schools are raising tadpoles, so the toadlets can be released at the nature centers.

Frogs that lay eggs in part-time ponds live in nearby forests. They travel to the pools each spring to lay eggs. Sometimes they are killed when they try to cross busy roads.

WOOD FROG

Frogs don't know that roads are dangerous, and drivers can't always stop in time. In some towns, people watch for wood frogs on warm, rainy nights in early spring. When they see migrating frogs, the caring citizens stop traffic while the frogs hop across the road.

When people make the trip safer, frogs can live and grow.

Some frogs can only survive in sunny, open woodlands.

GOPHER FROG

At one time, natural wildfires regularly burned back the plants in places where gopher frogs live. But when people settled in the area, they put out the flames. Without fire, some plants grew larger than ever before. They crowded out the smaller plants gopher tadpoles depend on for food and shelter. In spring, the big plants sucked up wetland water before tadpoles could develop into frogs. When scientists noticed the problem, they began to carefully burn some forest areas so gopher frogs can survive.

When people work to restore these wild places, frogs can live and grow.

Other frogs depend on wetlands surrounded by thick, low shrubs.

When people work to save these watery worlds, frogs can live and grow.

PINE BARRENS TREE FROG

In the late 1950s, a county planning board in New Jersey proposed cutting down a pineland forest to build an airport. The project would have destroyed dozens of ponds where Pine Barrens tree frogs live. Fortunately, scientists and citizens worked together to stop the project and protect the land forever. Thanks to their efforts, Pine Barrens tree frogs will always have a place to live.

many frogs live on land that is perfect for building homes and growing crops.

CALIFORNIA RED-LEGGED FROG

At one time, California red-legged frogs were easy to find. But many died as people cleared land to grow crops in the Central Valley. More died as people drained wetlands to build homes and businesses in Southern California.

In 2010, the U.S. Fish and Wildlife Service came to the rescue. It protected 1.6 million acres of land for the frog. In 2014, the California red-legged frog became the state frog. Now scientists are hoping it can make a comeback.

When people protect these natural areas, frogs can live and grow.

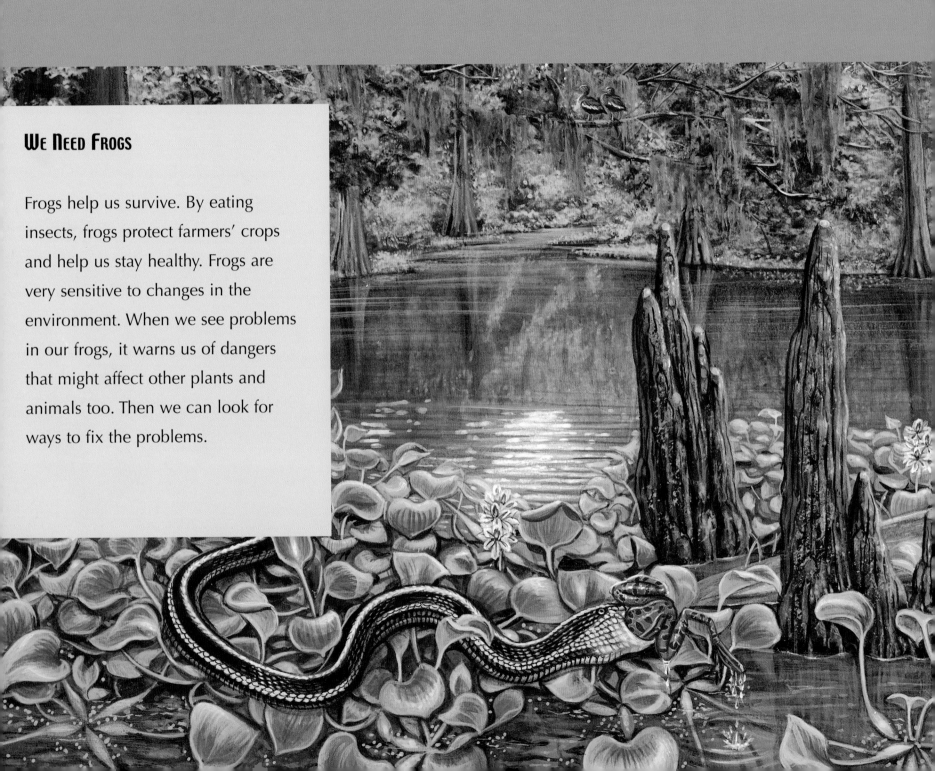

When too many frogs die, other living things may also have trouble surviving.

WE NEED FROGS

Frogs help us survive. By eating insects, frogs protect farmers' crops and help us stay healthy. Frogs are very sensitive to changes in the environment. When we see problems in our frogs, it warns us of dangers that might affect other plants and animals too. Then we can look for ways to fix the problems.

That's why it's so important to protect frogs and the places where they live.

OTHER ANIMALS NEED FROGS

Frogs are an important part of the food chain. Eggs and tadpoles are good sources of food for fish, large water insects, and ducks. Adult frogs are eaten by fish, snakes, lizards, bats, otters, foxes, water shrews, and birds. Without frogs, many other creatures would go hungry.

Frogs have lived on Earth for more than 200 million years.

HELPING FROGS

Do not catch and keep frogs. Let them live in their natural environment.

Do not buy frogs at a pet store. Frogs are wild animals and should live in their natural homes.

If someone gives you a frog, do not release it in a wild place. It could eat other frogs or make them sick.

Do not spray chemicals that could harm frogs.

Join a group of people that is keeping track of frogs that live in your area.

Sometimes people do things that can harm frogs. But there are many ways you can help these special creatures live far into the future.

Join a group of people working to protect or restore wetlands near your home.

Talk to teachers at your school about celebrating Save the Frogs Day. You can get more information about events happening near you at *https://www.daysoftheyear.com/days/save-the-frogs-day/*.

Frog Facts

* No one knows exactly how many kinds of frogs live on Earth. So far, scientists have discovered and named almost five thousand different species.

* About five hundred kinds of frogs belong to a family called the "true toads." They have dry, scaly skin and spend more time on land than other frogs. That means all toads are frogs, but not all frogs are toads.

* The Amau frog is the smallest frog on Earth. It's about the size of a housefly. The goliath frog is the world's largest frog. It's as big as a rabbit.

* In winter, wood frogs bury themselves in leaves and freeze solid. In spring, the males attract mates with a call that sounds like a quacking duck.

* Panamanian golden frogs communicate with one another by waving their hands.

Selected Bibliography

"America's 10 Most Threatened Frogs and Toads." National Wildlife, April 2010. Available online at https://www.nwf.org/News-and-Magazines/National-Wildlife/Animals/Archives/2010/Most-Threatened-Frogs-US.aspx.

Beltz, Ellin. Frogs: Inside Their Remarkable World. New York: Firefly Books, 2005.

"California Red-Legged Frog Named State Amphibian." California Department of Fish and Wildlife News, July 15, 2014. Available online at https://cdfgnews.wordpress.com/2014/07/15/california-red-legged-frog-named-state-amphibian.

"California Red-legged Frog." Los Padres ForestWatch, 2013. Available online at http://lpfw.org/our-region/wildlife/california-red-legged-frog.

Goddard-Taylor, Gayle. "Habitat Rebirth." Sanctuary, Spring 2014, pp. 12–14.

Lee, Jane J. "African Clawed Frog Spreads Deadly Amphibian Fungus." National Geographic, May 16, 2003. Available online at http://news.nationalgeographic.com/news/2013/13/130515-chytrid-fungus-origin-african-clawed-frog-science.

Meyer, Elizabeth. "A Head Start." AMC Outdoors, September/October 2014, p. 11.

Moore, Robin. In Search of Lost Frogs: The Quest to Find the World's Rarest Amphibians. Buffalo, NY: Firefly Books, 2014.

"Panamanian Golden Frog." Denver Zoo. Available online at http://www.denverzoo.org/animals/panamanian-golden-frog.

Rick, Relyea A. "New effects of Roundup on amphibians: Predators reduce herbicide mortality; herbicides induce antipredator morphology." Ecological Applications, March 2012, pp. 634–647.

Recommended for Young Readers

Bishop, Nic. Frogs. New York: Scholastic, 2008.

Guiberson, Brenda Z. Frog Song. New York: Holt, 2013.

Jenkins, Martin. Fabulous Frogs. Somerville, MA: Candlewick, 2016.

Markle, Sandra. Toad Weather. Atlanta: Peachtree, 2015.

Simon, Seymour. Frogs. New York: HarperCollins, 2015.

Acknowledgments

The author wishes to thank Andrew Blaustein, Professor of Zoology and Director of the Environmental Sciences Graduate Program, Oregon State University; John F. Bunnell, Principal Research Scientist, New Jersey Pinelands Commission; John Jensen, Senior Wildlife Biologist, Georgia Department of Natural Resources; Jeff Miller, Conservation Advocate, Center for Biological Diversity; Christopher Pearl, Wildlife Biologist, USGS-Biological Resources Division, Forest and Rangeland Ecosystem Science Center; Vance Vredenburg, Research Scientist, Museum of Vertebrate Zoology, University of California, Berkeley; and Bryan Windmiller, Grassroots Wildlife Conservation, Concord, Massachusetts, for taking time out of their busy schedules to discuss projects that are protecting frogs and preserving their habitats.

The illustrator gratefully acknowledges John F. Bunnell, John Jensen, and Dirk J. Stevenson for supplying photos used as reference for illustrations in this book.

RANGE
GREEN FROG

RANGE
NORTHERN
LEOPARD FROG

RANGE
SIERRA NEVADA
YELLOW-LEGGED FROG

RANGE
PANAMANIAN
GOLDEN FROG

All range boundaries are approximate.

RANGE
EASTERN
SPADEFOOT TOAD

RANGE
WOOD FROG